ENDURANCE

THE 7 SECRETS TO OVERCOME ANY OBSTACLE

KENDRA FIPPS CROWE

ENDURANCE
The 7 Secrets to Overcome Any Obstacle

Copyright © 2021. Kendra Fipps Crowe

All rights reserved. No part of this publication may be reproduced, distributed, or transmitted in any form or by any means, including photocopying, recording, or other electronic or mechanical methods, without the prior written permission of the copyright holder, except in the case of brief quotations embodied in critical reviews and certain other noncommercial uses permitted by copyright law.

Cover and Interior Design by
Transcendent Publishing

ISBN: 978-0-578-39448-0

Printed in the United States of America.

DEDICATION

To my Adrian and Andrea,

You both gave me much insight into who I needed to become.

I am so much stronger, wiser, and at peace because of you.

To my mom – you are truly one of my greatest inspirations. You showed me how to love and meet people right where they are with no judgments.

To my husband, Andrew – the Lord knew I needed a man with huge hands to catch me when I fall and a big heart where love for me grows more each day. That's why He gave me you.

Thank you all…

CONTENTS

Introduction vii

Chapter One: It's What You Know, Not Who You Know 1

Chapter Two: Forgiveness is the Key for You and Me 17

Chapter Three: Loving Yourself Through Your Pain 29

Chapter Four: Your Greatest Struggles Become Your Greatest Miracle 41

Chapter Five: A House Built on Quicksand 53

Chapter Six: A Roadmap to the Best Version of You! 67

Chapter Seven: God's Grace and Love 83

Chapter Eight: Never Give Up! 95

Bonus Chapter: How My Mentors Have Influenced Me 105

Recommended Reading 117

About the Author 119

INTRODUCTION

If I asked you to picture a marathon, you'd probably envision participants of all backgrounds, skill levels, and physical builds. Some have trained for years, some months, others for weeks. Each has a variety of experiences and motivations that have led them to this race. However, they all share the same dream: crossing the finish line first.

Of course, only one person will do so; many will finish seconds or minutes later, while others will bring up the end or not finish at all. Why does this happen? What separates some runners from others? The answer is that success doesn't always come to those who start off the fastest or the strongest, but rather those who are able to endure, staying committed to their goals even when their road gets rough.

The concept of endurance is one that applies to every area of life. We can see the evidence of this in the lives of successful men and women who consider their persistent nature to be their greatest strength. In this book, we will unravel limiting mindsets and explore approaches on how to boost your own endurance in the marathon of your life.

Consider this interesting fact: according to researchers, if a sprinter kept running in the opposite direction of their destination, they would still inevitably arrive there (though it may take a bit longer). This is possible because the globe is round, meaning that our end will always lead us back to our beginnings.

This is not just a piece of trivia, but the foundation of why just about anything can be achieved with endurance. Defined by the determination found in the period between hard work and eventual achievement, endurance is truly one of God's greatest gifts to humanity.

No matter what you set out to achieve, endurance is the vehicle to get you there. It is through endurance that drops of water gradually turn into ponds, rivers, and ultimately the mighty ocean. Through the act of endurance, the greatest turbulence gradually becomes a soothing calm. And with a mindset of endurance, seemingly daunting challenges can be transformed into child's play.

Are there situations that you feel are impossible to overcome? Are you having difficulties with your child(ren) or in your relationship or finances?

Do you feel far away from the glorious picture you once painted for your future? Do not be troubled! Your situation is about to turn around for your highest good. You'll soon look back at these challenges in awe, because through use of your endurance you are becoming aligned with the best version of your victorious self!

In the pages ahead, you will learn how to overcome any obstacle from within. You will learn how to balance your relationships, family, and business with ease through the Art of Endurance.

How can I make this promise? Because I believe you were led to this book for a reason. It probably means you are at a place in

INTRODUCTION

your life where you're ready to make a change. Or perhaps you're reading it because you wanted to support me. Maybe it's a bit of both. Whatever the case, I'm so grateful that we get to hang out for a while, and that I have the opportunity to provide you with a deep dive into how you can harness the power of endurance – and, hopefully, entertain you as well.

I wasn't born with a silver spoon in my mouth. And, like most of you, I had to fight for what I have today. Nothing is ever given to you without a price attached to it. Freedom comes when you have paid the price yourself; liberation comes when you are living your passion every day.

I grew up in the South, and in many ways had what I would say was a privileged childhood. My siblings and I were bought up by a single woman with a strong right hand and a loving heart. Our mom is one of the strongest women I know. She raised us to be strong, independent, self-sufficient, generous, and extremely compassionate towards others.

In other ways, my childhood was more challenging than most can imagine. Many of you holding this book knows someone from the South, or maybe your family migrated from the South. At one point in this country's history, more than one million people did so, thinking they would have an easier life elsewhere. My grandparents decided to stay and raise their kids on a plantation, so you might say our family knows a bit about hard work! They found ways to make the little they had go a long way. We never went to bed hungry, even if we had greens for breakfast the next day.

I've never been afraid of hard work. When I was young, picking and chopping cotton for my school clothes was the only option I had. I promised myself that if I got out, my own kids would never live like this. If this is completely foreign to you, I understand. Just imagine a group of people moving down a row of six-foot-high plants, plucking white fluffy balls of cotton as fast as they can, and shoving them in bags on their shoulders. Well, I was one of them... at least for a while. You see, I wasn't filling my bag fast enough and decided to toss in the green bulbs of cotton, which were not ready to open, to give it weight. Talk about a plan that went wrong. My mother was told never to bring me back and I learned two valuable lessons: life is about owning up to your mistakes, and there are no shortcuts.

When I trace back to what has made me the woman that I am today, it's endurance. Life is going to throw hardship, heartbreak, financial setbacks, illness, and even death your way. But when you can embrace all of those things and live with true happiness in your heart, you have mastered the Art of Endurance.

For a very long time, I lived with self-doubt, self-pity, insecurities, doubting myself, and not feeling loved. That all ended the day I found myself sitting in a hospital room beside an eight-and-a-half-month-old baby fighting for his life.

A year prior to giving birth to my son, I was on track to receive a full-ride basketball scholarship at a local community college. My dream was to play professional basketball. Once I became a mother, my life was no longer about me; it was about being a voice for the voiceless. It was finding the strength from within to provide for him. Now, I listened in disbelief to the team of doctors discussing how this baby, who had been born healthy, might not survive after contracting a virus and suffering three strokes. All I remember is saying, "Lord, help my son. I promise to stay with him and provide for him for the rest of his life. Whatever comes our way I will get through it. God, just give me strength to endure."

That moment marked a turning point; it was when I began learning how to overcome any obstacle in my life. Reading this book could be that turning point for you. If you intend to skim through it without being open to the possibilities of repairing relationships, forgiving yourself, or finding a way to have a deeper relationship with your God, then you're saying yes to that insanity of doing the same thing over and over and expecting change. If you really want to transform your life, then bring your A-game, bring an open mind and, most importantly, bring yourself.

Use this text as a companion and guided reflection to help you build your endurance and train your mind to welcome in your new reality. I'll be with you every step of the way, and I can't wait to meet you at the finish line!

CHAPTER ONE

IT'S WHAT YOU KNOW, NOT WHO YOU KNOW

"Whenever you're in conflict with someone, there is one factor that can make the difference between damaging your relationship and deepening it. That factor is attitude."

- William James

Romance between two people is a sweet thing that creates a feeling of confidence in their minds and fullness in their hearts. For many, it feels so good (and maybe a bit of a relief) to have a companion to walk through life with.

It's never easy to stand alone; a single cord is easy to break. While an individual may struggle with life's challenges, a couple presents a united front, with each person pulling the other up and lending support in times of trouble.

As awesome as new love can be, however, we usually get little time to enjoy it before we're hit by bitter realities we didn't anticipate. This typically causes us to question if we ever previously "knew" our partner at all.

The truth is that we all come across stumbling blocks in our romantic relationships sooner or later, and our exposure (gradual or sudden) to the various aspects of the people we care about can be challenging for us to accept and acknowledge.

For some people, these hidden truths are a buried past that creep in to seemingly ruin hope for the future. Traumas from childhood or past relationships can destroy a person's emotional balance and alter their energy at times. For others, meeting the demands of their personal ambitions as well as being present for their partners is a constant battle.

Career women tend to find marriage especially challenging, partly because many men still prefer women who are submissive to their whims. The idea of a woman going all out to earn a living may make her partner jealous or suspicious, which can be difficult to navigate. When these women have children, they are presented with even more obstacles. They often become torn between honoring their wifely duties and pursuing their careers while also simultaneously providing their kids with the care and attention they need.

I remember when a friend joined the company where I was working. Her husband didn't support this; she also had four small kids and a side business she worked in addition to her full-time job. They were barely making ends meet, yet her husband complained she was falling behind in her family duties. The food was cold, the kids weren't being bathed on time, and the house was a mess. He told her to quit her side business, and when she refused, he took her laptop computer smashed it on the floor. She was crushed emotionally; all she wanted to do is help him provide for the family. She "just wanted to make things easier for him," she said. Little did her husband know that she continued running her business from her cell phone. She started to make extra money and lots of it. When he found out her husband said, "I knew you could do it." Some of us get supportive spouses and some of us must prove to our spouses that it's possible before getting that support. It never feels good to fail; however, we get past it when we realize this can be a learning experience, a seed to get you closer to success. Supporting your spouse regardless of current circumstances will help them learn from failures to grow into a beautiful lioness or lion.

Your Past Should Never Determine Your Future

In the face of fierce challenges, our ability to think clearly and keep our eyes on the finish line often disappears. It is easy to lose focus when we feel that the life we've always dreamed of is out of reach. You must remember, though, that focus is one of the critical ingredients of endurance. When we lose focus, we are unable to sustain the direct energy required to achieve extraordinary feats.

Ludwig Van Beethoven, one of the most famous composers of all time, began losing his hearing in his twenties. Yet he continued to work; in fact, he wrote his most popular piece, "Für Elise," when he was already severely impaired, and six symphonies after becoming completely deaf. In total, he would compose more than seven hundred pieces. Imagine what that had to be like for him, imagine the comments of naysayers and other obstacles he had to overcome. Imagine what would have happened if he had given up when his hearing started to fail. Not only would he have lost his passion in life, but the world would have missed out on some of the most beautiful music in history.

Stevie Wonder is another musical phenom who, despite his blindness, has had massive success from singing, playing instruments, and writing music for others.

People told the young Albert Einstein, "You'll never amount to anything in life," because he was believed to be the dullest student in school and diagnosed as dyslexic. Today he is revered as one of the most brilliant physicists who ever lived.

1 | IT'S WHAT YOU KNOW, NOT WHO YOU KNOW

The unifying truth in all these scenarios (and the millions more like them) is this: Your current position and your past can't limit you from attaining great heights, if it is your will to do so.

You must believe in yourself, be disciplined, and not be easily discouraged by the way your circumstances appear. To feed into disbelief is to pollute and dilute your efforts. All the aforementioned great achievers had something in common: they were all of the belief that the material conditions of their present were not a reliable predictor of their future.

Liberate yourself of any limiting ideas. Add more positivity to your life by associating with positively thinking people. They can be identified as those who encourage you to give your best, and add a little extra effort. Their presence should inspire you to stretch yourself beyond your perceived limits.

If instead you find yourself in a circle of people who are fond of talking down on your goals, or consistently comment on how "bad" you are as opposed to affirming you, then you should consider changing the company you keep. Align yourself with those who want the best for you, so that you may be aligned with your highest self.

Remind yourself, "If I believe it, I can achieve it. If I believe it, I will become it." Know that you can and will become everything you desire to be. Yes, you can!

A large part of being able to endure is your conviction. Ultimately, it's all about believing. Each failure plants a seed for success. However, just like a farmer might decide to harvest his seeds or replant them, we too can interpret our failures negatively and fall into resentment, or we can learn from them and use the lessons gained to produce different and better future outcomes. Should we choose the latter, we can be certain that success is closer with each new attempt to achieve our goals.

Let's take a look at a fantastic example that'll better illuminate this idea: If you were to fail a test or lose a job, it's safe to assume you would feel some regret. You may attribute your failure to your poor preparation; you may blame your anxiety, or you may believe you took the wrong approach to answering the questions. Whatever you view as the source of your failure does not matter. It is what you do after the loss that makes or breaks you.

If you choose to take the test again, you may choose to be more prepared, calmer, and more informed, or you may choose to call off the test entirely. After an experience such as failing, both decisions would be justified. The key is to examine the motivations behind the decisions. Deciding to retake the exam may result from wanting to achieve something greater. Choosing to forego the exam may be due to the shame or embarrassment you felt and/or the fear of falling flat again.

In the case of losing a job, getting yourself up to find and explore better employment opportunities will eventually lead to smoother roads for your personal journey. Sulking, however, will not only distract you from focusing on a better circumstance, but the energy generated from such negative thoughts will naturally drive better offers away from you.

You must see failures as setups for success. If something does not yield a positive result in your first trial, do not quit. Know that success is inevitable in the end, put in the sustained effort, and do your best to fulfill all the conditions required of you. Remain disciplined in your pursuits and be open to discovering areas where you made errors and learn from them. Once you apply your findings, you will experience success faster than you previously imagined. As it says in Proverbs 24:16, "For though the righteous fall seven times, they rise again, but the wicked stumble when calamity strikes."

Take Responsibility for Your Personal Growth

Once upon a time, *someone* informed *everyone* that it was *everyone's* duty to do the task assigned. Upon discovering this, *some* decided that since it was *everyone's* duty, *anyone* could do it. Eventually, *everyone* left the task to *anyone* to do it and, in the end, who did the job? You guessed it: *no one*.

This short story explains that when we leave our duties for other people to do, they end up either undone or, perhaps even worse, not done well.

The duty of ensuring that you continue growing in every area of your life is chiefly yours! You can choose to ignore your responsibilities or shove them in the hands of someone else. You may even assume that paying a psychologist, a counselor, or seeking out an adviser or a mentor might relieve you of accountability, but the truth is no one holds the key to your destiny except you.

Always take responsibility for your growth. Compare how much better you are today, intellectually, than yesterday. If you realize that you are declining in one way or another, you must help yourself build your capabilities and capacity to do and be more.

If you refuse to evaluate your personal growth you will lessen your chances of success. Your life's outcomes are the culmination of your personal choices. Make choices that support the life you envision living tomorrow, today, and watch your circumstances improve daily.

1 | IT'S WHAT YOU KNOW, NOT WHO YOU KNOW

Review Questions

What are some things from your past that you still carry with you today? How do you feel this incident or circumstance has affected who you are and what did that experience teach you?

_____
_____
_____
_____
_____
_____
_____
_____
_____
_____
_____
_____
_____
_____
_____
_____
_____
_____
_____
_____
_____
_____
_____
_____

ENDURANCE

1 | IT'S WHAT YOU KNOW, NOT WHO YOU KNOW

ENDURANCE

1 | IT'S WHAT YOU KNOW, NOT WHO YOU KNOW

Do you feel that you are responsible for every decision, and if so, why? Is there someone or a situation keeping you from reaching your full potential?

ENDURANCE

1 | IT'S WHAT YOU KNOW, NOT WHO YOU KNOW

ENDURANCE

CHAPTER TWO

FORGIVENESS IS THE KEY FOR YOU AND ME

"To forgive is to set a prisoner free and discover that the prisoner was you."

- Lewis B. Smedes

When was the last time you checked yourself into a hotel? If you're like most of us, before booking the rooms, you asked yourself things like: Can I afford it? Does it have the amenities I enjoy and is it in an area I want to stay? How many bags am I bringing with me, and how many nights will I be there? After making sure it has everything on your list, you make your choice.

You arrive to find that in luxury hotels, there is usually a doorman who is always ready to accommodate you and assist you with your luggage. When you get to your room, there is even a handwritten note welcoming you.

These days, I prefer the most perfect suite available. I enjoy and look for four- or five-star hotels with excellent amenities and the best customer service. However, at one point in my life I decided to check myself into the heartbreak hotel. I spent all my holidays, summers, and family vacations in this desolate building, where I experienced one disappointment after another. There was a doorman, but he was rarely available when I needed him; the maids barely cleaned the room or left fresh towels.

I'm sure you're wondering what I mean exactly… Well, being in and out of relationships took a toll on me; it was as if I had spent too much time visiting properties with only one- or two-star reviews. So many of my friends had similar experiences, locking themselves up in isolation because of the trauma they had incurred from broken relationships.

I continued living in this sad state for a long time, until one day I noticed that a great financial crisis had my "hotel." The doorman was gone, and I had to open the doors myself. The maids now only tidied up once a week, and there was a growing odor that even the carpet freshener couldn't mask. And the room that had once felt warm and comfortable was now revealed to be dingy and depressing. I realized it had always been this way; I had simply been overlooking these truths to remain a resident of this place, which was actually a prison created by my toxic romances.

I share this analogy because my occupancy at the heartbreak hotel wasn't the end of my story, or my love life. If you are in a bad relationship, or have just ended one, there is hope for you too! It's time to upgrade your amenities! My hotel was closed down; however, I can proudly say that it is now under construction, and under the supervision of new management.

In reality, it was a three-day retreat that changed everything for me. During my time in this safe space, I became aware that I was trapped in a story of which I was the sole author. From the time I was a little girl until that point, I had felt unloved. Growing into adulthood, I felt even more abandoned. My inner narrative became, "No one loves me, and so I will have to take care of myself." This included the belief that I couldn't trust any man, which probably stemmed from the broken relationship between me and my father.

This narrative persisted until I was in my late thirties. I came to realize that it wasn't the relationships that were so bad. It was my perspective! My poor self-image had caused me to suffer greatly, both internally and externally.

Just imagine putting two pairs of glasses on. Your vision wouldn't be so clear. It was like that when I went into relationships, already anticipating betrayal. With time, I got just that.

I had heard the saying, "When you heal the little girl, the women will appear." Inspired by this adage, I not only began to forgive people who had broken my heart, I also called a few of them and asked *them* to forgive *me*.

It's certainly not easy to ask for forgiveness. I, however, realized that taking responsibility for my role would start an in-depth healing process that would allow me to edit my story. I began to focus on the right parts of the relationships and what I learned. We are all made in the image of God. He created *everyone*, which means He loves them, and He loves me as well.

I, in turn and in time, learned to love myself. The good, the bad, and even the ugly parts all made for a perfect me. I learned imperfection is what makes all humans unique. Rather than remain in emotional isolation, I learned to outwardly celebrate my victories and even openly embrace my failures. I wasn't so hard on myself anymore. I also no longer gave credence to what people thought of me. I realized I am not selfish when I put myself first in the ways that matter; in fact, it benefits everyone, because then I can give from a full cup.

I realized too that I deserved to check myself into a "five-star hotel." I wrote down all the amenities I wanted and researched the property. Sure enough, I landed myself a very good man and began living what I had thought was an unbelievable fantasy.

Forgiving people is often difficult, but once you do it can help you heal very quickly. It can help you fill your own cup with a long-lasting joy that you can then share freely with others.

The message of my testimony is simple: let forgiveness flow freely through you and heal your broken heart. You will not only rise above whatever may be holding you down, you will be motivated and encouraged, both of which are vital to boosting your endurance.

Review Questions

Who do you need to forgive? Who would you like to forgive you? What's one thing you need to forgive yourself for before moving forward?

_____
_____
_____
_____
_____
_____
_____
_____
_____
_____
_____
_____
_____
_____
_____
_____
_____
_____
_____
_____
_____
_____
_____

ENDURANCE

2 | FORGIVENESS IS THE KEY FOR YOU AND ME

How many times did you land in the heartbreak hotel? Who helped you to get out? Are you grateful you got out? What lessons did you learn? Or, are you still there?

_____
_____
_____
_____
_____
_____
_____
_____
_____
_____
_____
_____
_____
_____
_____
_____
_____
_____
_____
_____
_____
_____
_____
_____
_____

ENDURANCE

ENDURANCE

CHAPTER THREE

LOVING YOURSELF THROUGH YOUR PAIN

"Owning our story and loving ourselves through that process is the bravest thing that we'll ever do."

- Brené Brown

It never feels easy to create happiness when you are going through pain. However, pain, like many things in this life, is all a matter of perspective.

If you choose to receive an unpleasant situation positively, you will surely mold a more positive outcome. This is most often demonstrated by the "cup half-full/half-empty" analogy. While two things can be true at the same time, an optimist will choose to focus on the cup's fullness as opposed to its lack. When it comes to applying this principle to others, we can extend grace to those we believe have hurt us by giving them the benefit of the doubt.

For example, if someone steps on your foot, is your first reaction to assume that they did so maliciously, or do you think they accidentally tripped? If you believe it was an accident, it's hard to feel anger towards the other person. The result is you get to maintain your sense of personal peace. Sure, optimists often have experiences that don't turn out the way they initially appeared; however, pessimists often preemptively project negativity onto events that don't have to turn out that way. The difference is the optimist can often create peace in any circumstance, whereas the pessimist tends to find conflict even where there isn't any.

To return to the subject of love, eventually it was time for me to move out of the hotel I had created in my head. As I began building a new home at the age of twenty-nine, I found myself fervently hoping and praying that my baby girl wouldn't end up like me.

Her father, like mine, wasn't in her life (a decision that was solely his). I never spoke ill of him, though; I would just say, "When you grow older, you will find out yourself. You must respect your father." Although some part of me wanted to find a father and husband for my children, another part assured me that, "I can do *bad* all by myself."

The need to save my daughter from the same pains I went through changed everything for me. I purchased a corner lot and the construction began on our new home. The kids and I would visit the property regularly. I believed that the house would give us a good start. The paint was fresh and the carpet too. Nothing smells better than a new home.

3 | LOVING YOURSELF THROUGH THE PAIN

Still, my self-esteem remained low. So many people would say to me, "Look how beautiful you are… No baby fat, no stretch marks, and no butt. You should be a model."

But their kind words fell on deaf ears. I didn't understand what they appreciated about me. Rather than searching for a way out of my depression, I was busy telling myself more negative things.

Later, I met this retired professor (I'll call him "Ed"). He saw right through my brave façade and gave me several books on rearranging my mindset.

One of the books (I wish I could recall which one) stated that we are all cosmically connected, therefore forgiveness is the key to true happiness. Rather than accepting the idea, I continued fighting the war within me. I told myself, "I am sure a situation like mine has never happened to the author of the book." In fact, I was actually *angry* with the author! Still, I continued reading, and as I did a particular woman kept coming to my mind. She had said some terrible things about me over a guy – something that made me furious. Then – and this was the strangest thing – I started running into her everywhere I went.

I saw her so many times that I finally decided to take the author's advice and forgive her. And as if by magic, I stopped seeing her! That's when I started to value what the author had to say. The book had shifted something for me, and I found myself being grateful for the things I read inside.

The book alone couldn't teach me how to love myself, but I did learn that on the road to doing so, being a grateful and content person with where you are is a perfect start!

3 | LOVING YOURSELF THROUGH THE PAIN

Review Questions

When was the last time you wrote or spoke about all the things you are grateful for? What are those things? Write your list below.

_____
_____
_____
_____
_____
_____
_____
_____
_____
_____
_____
_____
_____
_____
_____
_____
_____
_____
_____
_____
_____
_____
_____

ENDURANCE

# 3 | LOVING YOURSELF THROUGH THE PAIN

ENDURANCE

3 | LOVING YOURSELF THROUGH THE PAIN

If loving yourself is so important, do you have a positive self-image or a negative self-image? How did you rebuild your poor self-image of yourself? What steps are you taking to improve your self-confidence?

_____
_____
_____
_____
_____
_____
_____
_____
_____
_____
_____
_____
_____
_____
_____
_____
_____
_____
_____
_____
_____
_____

ENDURANCE

3 | LOVING YOURSELF THROUGH THE PAIN

ENDURANCE

CHAPTER FOUR

YOUR GREATEST STRUGGLES BECOME YOUR GREATEST MIRACLE

> *"There are only two ways to live your life. One is as though nothing is a miracle. The other is as though everything is a miracle."*
>
> –Albert Einstein

One major obstacle that gets people off track of their goals is any form of sickness. It is usually impossible to make a person follow a particular line of thought when such a person is experiencing any form of sickness or disease. Most of the time the individual is so thrown off by the incident that their life comes to a screeching halt.

This is one of the reasons why it is essential to always be connected to the Creator. The one who gives life. If you are having a form of ailment, you should spend time praying to God about it and seek medical counsel. Life doesn't happen to you, it happens for you.

Your health condition should not be criteria to stop enduring. Remember that the achievements you make after your endurance are a permanent thing, but your health condition is not permanent.

The sickness you are experiencing today will surely leave you if you pray and tell God about it, and if you seek medical treatment.

Those who truly intend to achieve optimal living should never submit themselves to limitations of any kind. Those limitations will become your greatest strengths. Just keep enduring and persevering until the very end.

Ask me how I know? I will share how my own personal journey of faith has kept me, my son, and my family safe.

Think about the worst thing that can happen. I experienced virtually the greatest height of tribulations.

My son was diagnosed with meningitis at the age of eight and a half months. He lost all of his mobility, speech, hearing, and sight, and was paralyzed on his left side. Before this, he was a healthy baby. He walked and talk. I can still hear him saying "mom and dad," as he raced down the hall in his stroller. He was super fast in it. There would be days when he would be walking behind me in his stroller, and when I would turn the light off in the hallway, the darkness in the hallway would get him to move quickly toward the light. I know it sounds terrible to some but I wish I had more days to see him run down the hall.

I'm so grateful for those memories. One thing I know about life is that change is always in front of us.

You see at that time he had two major strokes and a minor stroke. He was transported by ambulance to Children's Hospital about two and a half hours away from us. A team of white coats came into the room to share with me their treatment plan. They said, "Your son is really sick. We are unsure if he will make it. We administered a drug and will have to wait and see if it works. And if it does work, he will be mentally delayed and will need medical attention for the rest of his life. We give him only 11.5 years to live." I was alone at the time with no family in the room with me. All I could do is pray and ask God for help. What do you think should have happened at this point in my life?

Some of you may think that I should have given up on any possibility of having my son restored to health or ever living beyond the set age, but I didn't do that. Rather, I decided to cling on to God who answered my prayers. Now, my son is 29 years old.

At the time I was raising two kids (with one of them having special needs). I had several odd jobs, broken relationships, failed businesses, and inevitably lack of self-confidence. And here I am today, still touching people's lives through the inspiration of how I was able to overcome my own challenges.

This one scripture changed everything for me when I heard it in Sunday School. John 9:2-3: "His disciples asked him, Rabbi, who sinned, this man or his parents, that he was born blind? Neither this man nor his parents sinned," said Jesus, "but this happened so that the work of God might be displayed in his life."

That one scripture has kept me focused on my faith walk! You too can overcome and be confident in a future that you probably never thought you could have. If you have faith, great things are bound to happen! I could have focused on all of the things in life most parents look forward to such as losing his first tooth, attending school, graduating from high school, playing sports, his dating years, or how he won't ever be able to give me grandchildren. However, I decided to be thankful for what I do have. This is what I told myself: No one person's situation is the same. And if God entrusted you with him, surely He has a plan for your life and his life. So, stay connected to the Source that gives life.

Endurance is not looking at your situation as being hopeless. It's realizing you have the power to turn things around with God's help. This miracle God performs on a daily basis with my son has restored my faith, love, trust, and hope each and every day.

We are spiritual beings having earthly experiences, so don't miss out on becoming the best version of yourself. The world is waiting earnestly for your manifestation. Come out and shine, because no light shines under a bushel. You are made in His image! Go ahead and tap into your greatest potential.

I'm not overlooking the ups and downs, the doctor visits, emergency room visits, surgeries, and calls from the nurses. I just choose to see everything as a miracle.

Review Questions

What has been the greatest miracle in your life? What had been your greatest struggle (e.g., illness, death, children, marriage, family, or finances)? How did those experiences shape your current decision making? In what ways did you become stronger in the faith walk?

ENDURANCE

ENDURANCE

4 | YOUR GREATEST STRUGGLES BECOME YOUR GREATEST MIRACLE

How many miracles have you experienced in your own life? List them so you may reflect on how blessed your life truly is. This list will serve as catalyst to help you get over rough times in life.

_____
_____
_____
_____
_____
_____
_____
_____
_____
_____
_____
_____
_____
_____
_____
_____
_____
_____
_____
_____
_____
_____
_____
_____
_____

ENDURANCE

ENDURANCE

CHAPTER FIVE

A HOUSE BUILT ON QUICKSAND

"Accept yourself, love yourself, and keep moving forward. If you want to fly, you have to give up what weighs you down."

— Roy T. Bennett

Shame was one of the biggest reasons I was willing to check in those rinky-dink hotels. My first hotel stay ever was the roach motel, represented by the relationships I saw and had with my loved ones and family members.

I hid a lot of things from my mother, including my first pregnancy at the age of twenty. I felt a lot of fear and didn't want to disappoint her. I quietly wore big clothes, and I only talked with her when it was necessary. I planned to finish high school, go off to college and play basketball with no one the wiser, but that plan fell apart very quickly when my oldest sister let the cat out of the bag. Everything I'd worked so hard for went down the drain.

For about four years, the basketball court had been my life. Our team won the majority of our games, we won conferences, and became the district champs, with only one loss from the State Championship. My future had seemed so bright. Our little town was so excited, and they were super supportive of us. There were only two sports at our high school – football and basketball – I was the first to play ball in my family. Now, my pregnancy meant that I was no longer the golden child, the local hero. It was a big blow to me. I had always felt like I had something to prove.

Then tragedy struck. As I mentioned earlier, eight months into my son's life, he got sick. I noticed he was dragging his swollen feet one day, and he was holding his left arm close to him. He had a fever. I took him to the doctor, who said it was a cold and an ear infection — no big deal. But two weeks later, the fever came back.

This time I became angry at his doctor and decided to take him to get a second opinion. At that visit, the new doctor said, "I'm going to admit him." From that very moment, sadness and pain became a permanent part of my life. If I had brought him in earlier, would things be different?

I blamed myself for his illness for many years. Mary and Barry (my nicknames for sadness and pain) heckled and harassed me daily, but I couldn't continue to play the victim. My son needed me and I needed all my strength to care for him. There was only so much space my mind could lease out. So I wrote a letter to Mary and Barry – my version of an eviction notice. "You both have me second guess myself on every decision," I wrote, "My self-esteem is so low, I can't recognize myself." With them in my life, I lacked confidence and I constantly questioned my self-worth. I didn't believe I deserved to be happy. Now it was time for all that to end. There was no thirty-day advance notification;

I immediately escorted them out of my life. "Get your belongings and go, I no longer belong to you, I am now free! And take every single thing you came with because I won't let you back in."

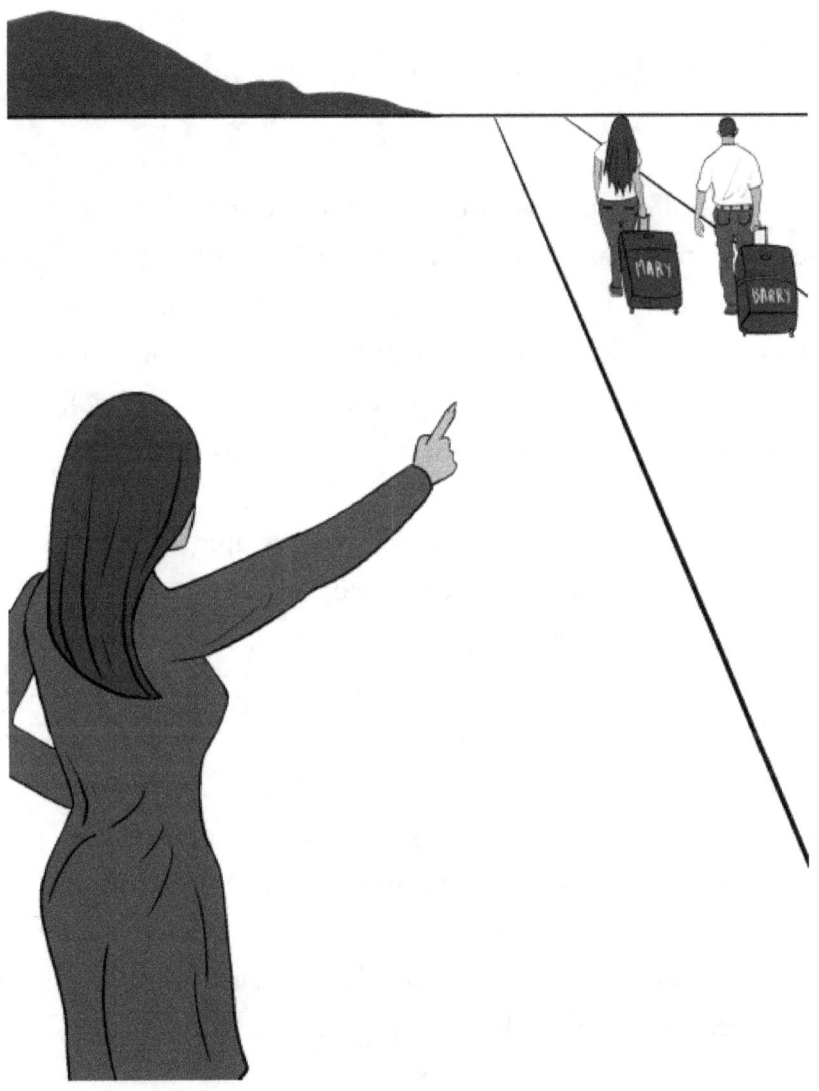

Letting Go of Other People's Opinions of You

Another challenge that often deters people from achieving their goals is the perception of or belief in their own inadequacy, also known as an "inferiority complex." Even though the majority of us present as having "self-control" and being confident and comfortable with our self-image, the truth is when we're confronted with the negative opinions of others we often internalize them.

Real control comes from our ability to ground ourselves in our personal truths and through implementing energetic boundaries for ourselves that serve as a buffer between our emotionality and others' reality. While not every criticism will be false or mean-spirited (no matter how difficult they may be to receive), most negative comments spoken out of malice are usually false.

For instance, someone might call you "'stupid" for not completing a task in the way they would, or perhaps disagree with your stance on a certain subject. However, we know that opinions are subjective and intangible; in other words, they literally and metaphorically hold no weight unless you allow them to. When reacting negatively to another's opinion of you, you must consider what its effect on you actually is. For example, does someone accusing you of being stupid magically transform your intellect? While your ego may be bruised, does their assessment of you physically hurt your body? Did it cause you to explode? Dissolve? Shrink into subatomic particles?

If the answer is no, then their opinions shouldn't matter in the tiniest bit. This takes the reinforcement of your mind with positive affirmations and constantly reminding yourself, "I am a person of worth. It doesn't matter if anyone else chooses to see or acknowledge that truth within me, I see and honor that truth within myself." For me, a source of struggle was others' perception of my son's condition and the resulting judgments I felt they made of me as his mother. During these times, I learned to console myself by adjusting my awareness and recognizing that the things being said to me were not of the person speaking them, but rather from some negative energy inhabiting them at that time. As discussed, that energy can take the form of many emotions (jealousy, sadness, anger, et cetera) that seek out other hosts to attack and make uncomfortable. (You know the saying "misery loves company."). What's important is we always have the choice to ignore it.

The best example I have found to illustrate this is Matthew 16:15 – 17. In the face of growing popularity and controversy surrounding Jesus' identity, He had asked His disciples, "Who am I?" While the others could not provide a credible answer, Peter, one of His most prominent and active disciples, replied, "You are Jesus Christ, the son of the living God." Jesus was extremely pleased, and responded, "Flesh and blood have not revealed this to you, but the *spirit of God within you.*"

Upon the realization of His impending physical death, Jesus relayed this information to this same group of disciples and a shocked and distraught Peter exclaimed, "Never! We wouldn't allow any such thing to happen to you." (Matthew 16:22-23) Jesus replied, "*I rebuke you, devil!*" referring to the conviction of Peter's statement.

Though Peter held no ill will towards Jesus, his sadness and disbelief (aka doubt) in the will of God at that time caused him to be inhabited by a different energy, a devil if you will, that allowed a lie to unknowingly fly from his lips. Though people don't always intend to be toxic, hurtful or lie, we are all dealing with whole universes inside of us. In other words, we are complex beings and not always aware of the influences that drive us and their effects on our relationships and/or the things we say. Regardless, if your interaction with anyone leaves you in mental, physical, or emotional pain, your primary responsibility is to preserve yourself. When you find yourself in those situations, separate yourself from them as soon as you can! If you attempt to stay, the person's negativity will inevitably consume and transform you too.

Review Questions

What's one thing you would do if you had no fear of another's judgment of you? In what ways do you find that you judge yourself? When did these beliefs about yourself start?

ENDURANCE

5 | A HOUSE BUILT ON QUICKSAND

ENDURANCE

5 | A HOUSE BUILT ON QUICKSAND

What types of emotions have you allowed to harass you daily? Was it regret, sadness, doubt, shame, guilt, or distrust? What caused you no longer want to be a victim? How were you able to pivot?

_____
_____
_____
_____
_____
_____
_____
_____
_____
_____
_____
_____
_____
_____
_____
_____
_____
_____
_____
_____
_____
_____
_____
_____
_____

… ENDURANCE

5 | A HOUSE BUILT ON QUICKSAND

ENDURANCE

CHAPTER SIX

A ROADMAP TO THE BEST VERSION OF YOU!

"It's not whether you have the willpower, it's whether you are ready to choose your best."

— Jackie Cantoni

I can remember how hard it was to get out of bed during this time in my life. I kept kicking myself for placing my son in a residential facility. I felt I had failed as a mother and went into a depression that lasted years. I remembered my son saying "Momma" once before he had his first stroke. After that, he never spoke again. The doctor told me and my mom to take him home and love him. They gave my son only eleven years to live. He is twenty-nine years old now and soon he will be thirty! Yes, over the years we did have some major medical scares with him. In the beginning I felt like God had cursed me and my son, only to find that I was destined to become the best version of me despite my circumstances. We all have the power to get through anything and come out on the other side, hopefully a better person. This is one of the greatest promises of endurance. First, though, you have to acknowledge where you are, accept where you are, and then pivot.

As mentioned previously, failures are merely stepping-stones to success. It is often true that successes we had to earn (after a series of losses) have more longevity and are more enjoyable than those delivered on a platter of gold. It is the difficulties you encounter on your road to becoming better that serve as catalysts for your arrival. One has to prioritize their sense of personal peace and not allow the circumstances of their past or their previous trials to embitter them. How then, does one "enjoy" the act of endurance?

1. Acknowledge God

In everything you do, always invite and acknowledge God, The Source, the Creator. The bible says in Proverbs 3:5, *"Trust in the Lord with all your heart and lean not on your understanding. In all your ways, acknowledge Him, and He shall direct your path."*

It is important to remember in this life that while we are the main characters of our individual stories, there is a bigger picture we are a part of and are being animated by an artist who is constantly adding to His masterpiece. Because we are not Him, we do not possess all the answers or know all the whys and wherefores of our lives; we can only trust that the end result will be something of beauty to behold. Acknowledgment and thanks for the colors and characters (both good and bad) are the keys to how we experience our lives. Think of it this way – we feel joy when our children boast about what we can do for them; it encourages us to do more. When they trust us enough to consult us before taking steps, we feel happy. Through prayer and a relationship with God we can reside within this same type of connection. Tell God about your plans and your desire to be a better version of yourself and voila! If it's in accordance with His will, He will honor your request. If you feel you've been rejected or kept from something that you've prayed for, then trust that like a good parent, God is redirecting your steps for something better. Remember that what you may perceive as a delay doesn't equate to a denial in the grand scheme of God's plan for your life.

2. Write the Vision and Make it Plain

On a piece of paper or your preferred notepad, write "How I Can Be a Better Version of Me?" Write things down that you feel need to improve. Do you need to read some books? Do you need to exercise? Do you need to find a new group of friends? Whatever it is, write it down and think about ways to approach these goals. Be sure you're being honest with yourself and make sure you don't hold back (because anything you push aside for later may become one of the most critical things you'll need to work on).

3. Chart Your Course

After completing your list, the next step is to contemplate and write out the step-by-step process to actualizing your goals. Consider the ways that your achievement might be hindered by bad habits or environmental factors and include steps you'll take if you need support or help. Maybe you'd benefit from an accountability partner? Maybe you'd do best to include a cheat day into your regimen? Whatever it is you're seeking to improve, always give yourself grace and remember to treat yourself with kindness.

4. Give Yourself Time to Grow

After you've written down the steps it'll take and visualized your best self, start assigning yourself checkpoints and/or timeframes in which you'd like to have certain objectives completed. Again, be gentle with yourself if they change or you don't meet each one.

5. Stay Focused

Distractions are bound to set in when you choose to become better. People around you may not get the message; they may even feel you are acting "weird." Even if you notice your circle changing or shrinking, keep going towards your desired outcome. With time, the smoke will clear and the people meant to leave and those meant to remain in your life will reveal themselves. Even though you will encounter changes and may falter slightly along the way, keep going! Remember, there are no limits. If you can dream it, you can achieve it. Is it a perfect home? Is it ideal health? Is it love? Whatever it is, when you set your mind to it, it will eventually be yours.

6 | A ROADMAP TO THE BEST VERSION OF YOU

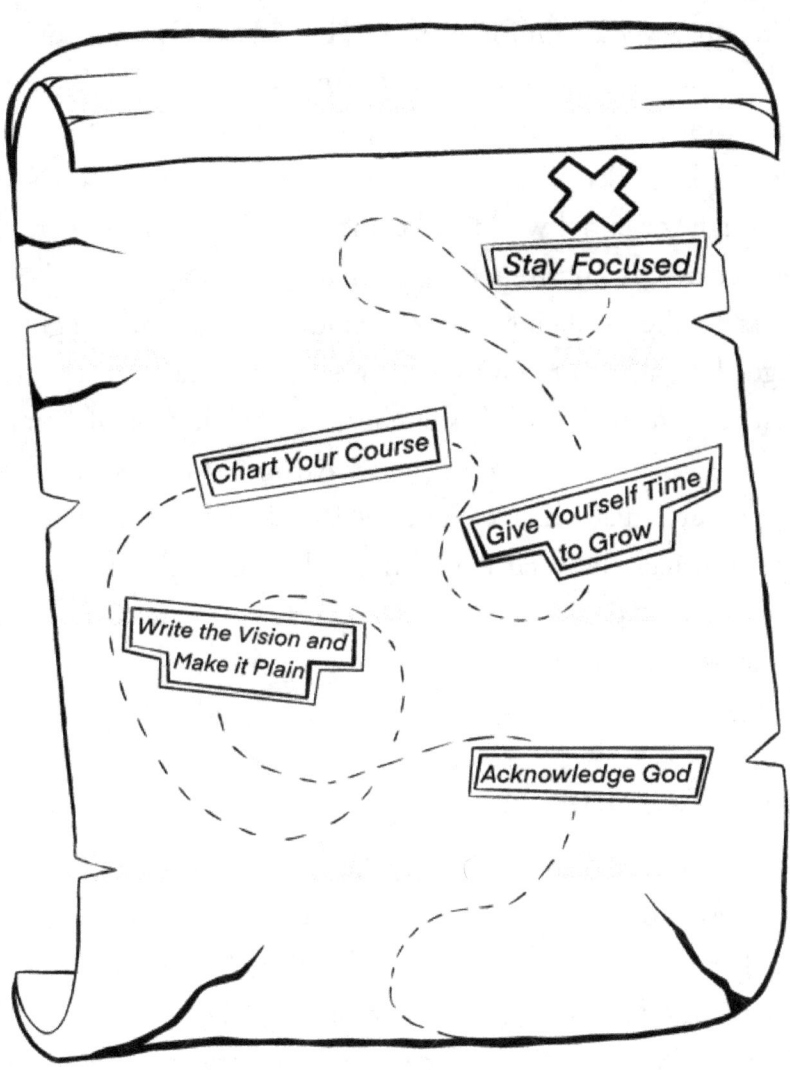

FACING FEAR

What is Fear?

There are several definitions of fear, but I have always resonated with the acronym "False Evidence Appearing Real." We all feel fear at some point (often various points) in our lives. When my son was diagnosed as an infant, I was devastated and afraid; I felt as though the entire world had come to an end. I know there are a lot of people confronted by similar circumstances; if it's not illness or the wellbeing of their children/child, they might be plagued by a fear of failure or even success. Whatever it is, you must remember that while some fears are valid, most are simply not true. Interestingly, researchers have agreed that 85% of our fears never actually happen, and 79% of the challenges that later happen usually have far fewer effects than anticipated, meaning that only 15% of the world's worries manifest and have the severe impact they portend.[*]

How do We Defeat Fear?

First, remember fear is a perception, a presumption that isn't often based on truth. It's just an idea you've built in your head that doesn't serve you. I'm reminded of the tale of a man who was walking in a dark corridor of his home when he suddenly froze in shock. He saw what he assumed was a phantom with a bloody mouth. Understandably, his first response was fear; he ran back into his room and jumped out of his bedroom window. As soon as he alerted the neighbors of what he had seen, the brave ones

---

[*] https://www.huffpost.com/entry/85-of-what-we-worry-about_b_8028368

escorted him back into his apartment with a torch. When they arrived at the corridor, they saw that the source of this moving phantom was simply a white piece of cloth that had a crimson tie crossed on it. The man had hung his shirt on a hook in the passageway and was afraid of his own creation.

A prevailing message throughout the bible is "fear not," and, indeed, many across the world find it beneficial to lean unto their faith during times of fear. Developing a spiritual practice and giving your worries/anxieties over to something greater than yourself does wonders for your physical and mental health. Unless turned into fuel, fear cannot help you achieve anything. You have been given all you need in this life and you are most certainly bigger than your fears. As it says in 2 Timothy 1:7, "For God has not given us a spirit of fear, but of power and of love and of a sound mind."

Finding Ways to Create Your Happiness

As you work toward becoming a better version of yourself it is essential to ask yourself where you are placing your focus in the name of being "happy." True happiness does not come from the accumulation of wealth or possessions. True happiness comes from a choice to remain positive and give your attention to the good things so they grow. In cultivating the garden of thoughts, try using the following tools to reap and sow happiness.

Appreciate What God Has Already Done for You

Those who are happy within do not pretend to be satisfied; they appreciate every little thing that the Creator has done for them. It's not that these people don't have reasons to be sad, but they develop and focus on a deep appreciation for what they know and feel God is doing in their lives. This is because they believe that everything God does is always good and always for their good. By reflecting on and appreciating this concept, joy grows and sustains them even in the face of hardships.

Know It's All Necessary

When something happens, it can be difficult to see the bigger picture. Things are only good or bad based on our interpretations of them. If we have that much power through the exercising of choice, why then would we choose to feel miserable? A deaf man may not be happy until he comes across a one-eyed man. On the other hand, the one-eyed man may not feel any contentment until he encounters one who is completely blind.

The truth is, no one's situation is worse than anyone else's; we all struggle and succeed according to our own life paths. Everything we go through is meant to craft us into who we are supposed to be as well as to unlock the reservoirs of strength and skill that we most certainly always need later on down the line. It is through divine grace that we are allowed to frame the details of our bigger picture in the ways that we see fit, all through how we choose to perceive our circumstances and their impact on us.

Review Questions

What's one thing you would do if you knew for a fact that you could not fail? How can you begin to live more fearlessly in your day-to-day life?

_____
_____
_____
_____
_____
_____
_____
_____
_____
_____
_____
_____
_____
_____
_____
_____
_____
_____
_____
_____

ENDURANCE

ENDURANCE

Let's create your own road map! Write things down that you feel need to improve. How is your relationship with God? Do you feel like your relationship needs improvement? Do you need to read some books? Do you need to exercise? Do you need to find a new group of friends? Who will become your accountability partner? How many times will you both meet? How much time are you willing to dedicate to this process? Six months, one year, or two years?

_____
_____
_____
_____
_____
_____
_____
_____
_____
_____
_____
_____
_____
_____
_____
_____
_____
_____
_____
_____

ENDURANCE

ENDURANCE

CHAPTER SEVEN

GOD'S GRACE AND LOVE

"God answers the mess of life with one word: Grace."

~ Max Lucado

Though many have tried to articulate it, no one can quantify the grace of God and the abundance of His intense love. Questions I often come across are, "Where is God in the time of my troubles?" and "If God is so filled with love and grace, why do injustices happen?"

I too shared this same sentiment when I received my son's initial diagnosis at eight months. My whole world came crumbling down, and it made me question God's love and whether I deserved it. I felt hate for myself and was in an especially dark place.

The essence of stormy seas is for us to appreciate the calm that follows. The importance of darkness is the appreciation of light. Can you imagine who we'd be if we had everything we wanted? Imagine not having any idea of what negative things are?

Imagine that we had light twenty-four hours a day, we had happiness in every area, and lived in a perfect haven, without having ever experienced all the evils of the world. Of course, if this was the case, the world would be a very dull place. What value would the beautiful things we know and cherish hold if there were no opposite things to make us appreciate their importance?

While there is beauty and bliss found in the midst of peace, we appreciate the Almighty even more when we realize He prevails in the midst of our troubles to save us and give us strength. Everything, as the bible says, "works together for the good of those who love Him." God's creations are beautiful and they are a direct reflection of His love.

Ecclesiastes chapter 3 reveals that everything has a "time and season." Though nothing lasts forever, the temporary nature of all the things we experience, good and bad, are part of the grand divine design. The fact that all things are temporary is also a testament to God's everlasting grace. It is through this grace that we can foster true happiness and contentment and keep happiness deep within our hearts.

Acknowledgment of God's grace and love are two keys to success that, should you choose to believe in them, can offer you a less stressed life in a stress-filled world. Everyone has just as much access to these as they want; the more open you are to receiving God's love, the more you will receive. As your heart fills and grows with God's love in equal measure, you will understand that this love is infinite and immeasurable. It is an eternally expansive experience.

7 | GOD'S GRACE AND LOVE

He Taught Me How to Love

I know men and women who have been heartbroken and deal with true trauma from their emotional wounds. While relationships of all types can cause distress for those involved in their dynamic, those in marriages tend to sustain the most pain.

As a woman who has had her own share of romantic and relationship trauma, I know just how impossible the word "love" might sound to those with shared experiences.

I also know from personal experience that we can learn to love again despite the circumstances of our past, so pull up a chair and let me share. I didn't know my father as a child. My mother never married, so I never saw them fall or be in love. As a result, I told myself going into each relationship that it wouldn't last. And most of the time it didn't. You see, I never took the time to work on me. I had been in a long-term relationship with this guy and he cheated. I know, you are wondering how I found out about it. The young lady called me and asked if we were dating. Before the call, I had plans to relocate and even marry him. That one phone call changed everything for me for the next fifteen years… until I came across Dr. Myles Munroe. His teaching on relationships, business and spirituality truly changed me. I had to learn how to become whole, separated, and unique. His YouTube videos and books helped me tremendously. I was able to overcome a lot of past hurts and mend some relationships. And now for something you are not going to believe: that guy who had cheated on me fifteen years earlier found his way back to me. We are happily married. We both had a lot growing up to do. And we did.

You might have been involved with a monster that treated you as though you were their prey. They may have abused you in ways you've yet to heal from or be able to share with the world. Yet, while it will take time, you can recover from the pains from such dehumanizing situations to find true love again!

7 | GOD'S GRACE AND LOVE

The first step is to embrace the fact that multiple things can hold true at the same time. Just because a situation didn't end the way you'd hoped, a single bad incident does not make the entire thing terrible. If you have been abused, though you may feel guilty for staying longer than you "should" have or accepting less than what you know you deserve, the fact that you lived through such a negative experience is something to be celebrated. It does *not* mean that all future situations will bear the same fruit.

When you hold onto negative experiences and the limiting beliefs they sometimes yield, you risk falling into the belief that others are happier than you, or becoming envious of those who appear to have the relationship you want. This can then result in your spreading gossip or engaging in other negative behaviors that do not reflect the real you. So how do you get out of your pool of misery and into love? The bible says, "*Draw near to God, and He will draw near to you.*" I acknowledged that God could help me heal again, and I decided to make Him my first love.

With that, it became easy to forgive my past offenders and develop a new heart that could better accommodate my new understanding of love.

Review Questions

How can you show yourself more love and grace? How can you extend more love and grace to others in your life?

7 | GOD'S GRACE AND LOVE

ENDURANCE

7 | GOD'S GRACE AND LOVE

What past experiences still haunt you today? Write down what caused you the most pain and why you choose to hold on to it? Acknowledgment, acceptance, release, and pivot begin the healing process.

_____
_____
_____
_____
_____
_____
_____
_____
_____
_____
_____
_____
_____
_____
_____
_____
_____
_____
_____
_____
_____
_____
_____

ENDURANCE

7 | GOD'S GRACE AND LOVE

ENDURANCE

CHAPTER EIGHT

NEVER GIVE UP!

"No pain that we suffer, no trial that we experience is wasted... all that we endure, especially when we endure it patiently, builds up our characters, purifies our hearts, expands our souls, and makes us more tender and charitable, more worthy to be called the children of God..."

— Orson F. Whitney

The objective and definition of endurance is to never give up. Why should anyone give up when they can achieve anything they set their mind to? The truth is, you'd spend more energy and time giving up mid-stride than finishing the race. Why is this? When you quit prematurely, you run the risk of developing a resistance to perseverance and, with time, may find yourself easily deterred in many areas of your life at the slightest inconvenience.

Remember, your situation could always be worse and there are many who despite having a set of circumstances even more difficult than yours still strive every day to make things better for themselves. If they don't succumb to defeat, neither should you. The more you try, the sweeter the victory when you achieve. Set your eyes on the target and do not lose focus, and you will soon find yourself achieving your goal.

For our last anecdote, allow me to recall the story of Jesus walking on water (Matthew 14:25-29). Peter had seen Christ walking on water and pleaded with Jesus to let him do the same. Christ beckoned to Peter to come to Him, and it was while Peter was walking on the gentle waves that he became distracted and began to submerge. Imagine what Peter must've seen when he turned his eyes away from Christ? The sheer miracle of treading on the water as if it was a solid surface must have scared him, and so, consumed with confusion and disbelief, he lost focus and began to sink.

The same thing applies to us today. When you take your eyes off the big prize, you begin to submerge in the midst of your challenges. Be wise and stay alert! You are a few steps from your eventual victory. Do not give up now.

My faith has kept me focused, and you too can overcome and be confident of a future you probably never thought possible if you just stay your course. If you have faith, great things are bound to happen!

We are spiritual beings having earthly experiences, so don't stop yourself from feeling the spectrum of all the things this life has to offer. Do not dwell in your sadness, but allow your emotions to come so that they can eventually go. Use the things you'd like to change about your life as motivation to put yourself in alignment with your greatest desires. The world is waiting earnestly for your manifestations. Come out and shine, because you are a gem! Go ahead and live like that.

To sum it up, endurance is the bridge between you and your eventual breakthrough. The pages of this book have revealed principles and practices to increase your level of endurance so that you don't grow weary or weak at the edge of your success. Hopefully this message will help you discover the true riches embedded in your being. You are unique and deserve all the love you desire. Go ahead and live life. You were created by a loving and graceful God that wants the best for you and the best of you!

Review Questions

What walking on water miracle have you experienced in your life with God? Make a list of all the times He saved you from people, hurt, harm, or danger? Did He heal you or your family for a major illness?

_____
_____
_____
_____
_____
_____
_____
_____
_____
_____
_____
_____
_____
_____
_____
_____
_____
_____
_____
_____
_____
_____

ENDURANCE

I can't tell you how many times I've had my Peter moments. No one can ever say that Peter didn't encourage us from a doubter to believer to becoming one of the well-known crusaders or leaders of Christianity. So, today I challenge you to think about your own Peter moment. How did you persevere? How did you overcome? Finally, how did you endure?

ENDURANCE

ENDURANCE

BONUS CHAPTER

HOW MY MENTORS HAVE INFLUENCED ME

"A mentor is someone who sees more talent and ability within you, than you see in yourself, and helps bring it out of you."

—Bob Proctor

One may be pushed to ask: do our mentors play any role in the experience? I've consistently talked about God as the alpha and the omega (the beginning and the end) of our enduring experience. However, the short answer to the question earlier posed is 'yes.' Our role models play a very vital role in how well we persevere.

While working towards achieving any form of greatness, it is important as said in the first chapter of this book, to always do away with people who influence us negatively.

While doing this, we may soon realize that the heart cannot be blank for a very long time, so it is therefore essential to fill the blank spaces initially filled with the people who do not fuel our passion with people who can do that. No one else can fuel your passion more than a mentor in that field.

Maya Angelou mentored Oprah Winfrey. What a great pair! Two of my favorite people.

Yes, it's true – even Oprah had a mentor! Ms. Winfrey shares how Maya supported her, "She was there for me always, guiding me through some of the most important years of my life. Mentors are important, and I don't think anybody makes it in the world without some form of mentorship."

Mentors are people who have lived in the light of the path we have now chosen to live. Through their own experiences, we can gain a lot and be encouraged when we are confronted with the toughest challenges.

Good mentors are usually God's human representatives in our lives. We can pattern our lives according to theirs in order to be better than them. When we come across stumbling blocks, they are always there to show us how things had gone wrong and they lead us to the right path.

I cannot end this chapter without talking about the role mentors played in my life. When I was down, I counted on my mentors to draw me out from my pit of depression. It was usually as though they were experiencing the same things as me. They knew what I was going through because they had been there themselves. Naturally, the road would have been tougher to tread if it had not been for their guidance serving as a light on the journey.

However, it is important to remember that you are only to obey and follow your mentors only to the extent of which their values align with your values. Apostle Paul in the Bible strongly warns his followers: "Follow me as I follow Christ." Christ was one man who took twelve disciples and changed the landscape of the world with Christianity. His leadership style has been used as a great example for so many to follow. His teaching left instructions, parables, and visible proof that we all need a mentor. Not only did he perform miracles, but his apostles did as well.

All mentors are human, so please don't put them on a pedestal. If you observe an unruly behavior in your mentor, or if you discover that a person who should have been a good mentor has taken negative steps, you may consider this old adage, "garbage in garbage out." You are not looking for perfection, you are looking for guidance and support in a particular area in your life. Also, if you are convinced that your mentor has poorly advised you, seek mentoring from another older and more experienced mentor. If you don't agree with this mentor entirely, it is perfectly okay to get another person's perspective on it.

As a matter of fact, when you decide to take someone as your mentor, you should immediately inquire about their own mentor too, so that when they take a wrong step, you can consult their mentors for assistance.

Mentors can be seen in or encountered in religious houses (including matured clergymen in church or mothers in the church), around the families (matured elders in your family such as grandmothers or grandfathers), or corporately (professors or CEOs), etc.

I have had the best experience with my mentors. I worked alongside a seven-figure income for more than a decade. He introduced me to several of his mentors. For every course or conference he attended, I was able to be in the room with most of them. His ability to grow massive teams all over the world and support them at the same time gave me insight into what makes a great leader.

My first day meeting my mentor, I asked if he had an assistant. He said he did. I told him, "One day I will work for you and you won't be able to get rid of me." Fast forward until now, we are still great friends, and I can call him my brother.

Mentors come in all shapes and sizes. I have had mentors who didn't look the part. I'm sure you're familiar with the old adage: don't judge a book by its cover. Well, early on in my thirties I prejudged so many people. If they were not successful, then they were not useful to me. I had to learn several hard lessons because I wouldn't listen to sound advice. So, whatever you do, learn from or lean on people who have gone before you. Financial status is not the true sign of success. It's about finding true happiness and fulfillment in the now, which is often called the present.

I believe you need several mentors. I was blessed with a spiritual mentor as well. The day before I was getting ready to place Adrian in a residential care facility, we were attending a party. This pastor walks up to me and said, "God, told me you are going to place your son in a home, and I should go with you." The amazing thing about this is that no one at the party knew what I was about to do. I felt alone, scared, and truly sad about the decision. Yet, there was God once again ready to help me in my time of need. I didn't question what she said. So, the next day we traveled to the facility along with my spiritual mentor. The pastor was there for my son and me. She prayed over us the entire time. Most mentors come into your life for a season, while other mentors stay for a lifetime. Therefore, be open to mentors who can help you with your business, personal life, spiritual walk, health, and finances.

The best decision I made was to shut up and listen to my mentors. You don't always have to agree with them; however, your life can go so much smoother if you are willing to be mentored. I still have mentors currently in my life now. And you should also.

Review Questions

What have you dealt with in the past that you if had a mentor it could have turn out differently? Are you currently dealing with same situation? Make a list of areas in your life where you can still use a mentor now?

___

BONUS CHAPTER: HOW MY MENTORS HAVE INFLUENCED ME

ENDURANCE

BONUS CHAPTER: HOW MY MENTORS HAVE INFLUENCED ME

What areas of life you feel it is too private to let a mentor in? How do go by getting the support you need to get on the other side of that ordeal? What step are you taking to improve your situation without the aid of a mentor?

_____
_____
_____
_____
_____
_____
_____
_____
_____
_____
_____
_____
_____
_____
_____
_____
_____
_____
_____
_____
_____
_____
_____

ENDURANCE

BONUS CHAPTER: HOW MY MENTORS HAVE INFLUENCED ME

ENDURANCE

RECOMMENDED READING

This was one of the hardest lists to put together. There were so many authors who have influenced me. You can add this shortlist to your library by simply visiting Amazon.

I hope you will enjoy these books as I have for years.

Bible

Being Happy by Andrew Matthews

Waiting and Dating by Myles Munroe

The Alchemist by Paulo Coelho

The Greatest Secret in the World by Og Mandino

Inner Voice: Unlock Your Purpose and Passion by Russ Whitney

Unshakeable: Your Financial Freedom Playbook by Tony Robbins

The 48 Laws of Power by Robert Greene

The Warmth of Other Suns by Isabel Wilkerson

The Seven Spiritual Laws of Success by Deepak Chopra

ABOUT THE AUTHOR

Kendra Fipps Crowe is a business coach and Amazon-bestselling author who is passionate about helping others overcome their fears and become the best version of themselves. Kendra's own endurance journey began with a chance meeting with a retired professor. At the time she was working as an executive assistant and program coordinator for Amateur Swing, a golf clinic for underprivileged youth sponsored by a local nonprofit. It was also a low point for her in terms of self-image and self-worth. The professor saw something in Kendra she didn't see herself and gifted her with three books on self-improvement. Soon after this encounter she became a certified life coach, which served as her springboard into marketing and team-building.

A Mississippi native, Kendra currently lives in Belleville, Illinois with her husband and two dogs.

HAVE A QUESTION FOR Kendra?

Reach out to kendra@kendracrowe.com;
or kendra@sayyes2u.com

SOCIAL MEDIA

» Facebook: www.facebook.com/kendralfipps

» Instagram: www.instagram.com/kendrafippscrowe

» Twitter: www.twitter.com/kendrafipps

» Linkedin: www.linkedin.com/in/kendrafipps

SayYes2U
Is What The World Is Waiting For

My gift to you is a FREE Masterclass where I share these secrets and how to implement them into your life today to get results immediately.

Seats are limited and I am only looking to work with those who want to achieve maximum results immediately.

You will learn the seven secrets to:
- Getting unstuck
- Freeing yourself from past hurt
- Freeing yourself from resentment and trauma

All of this without hiring an expensive life coach. This works even if you have hired a coach and didn't get results.

Isn't it time you pivoted and endured through life's trials and tribulations? Register Now!!!!

SayYes2U.com

This Free Masterclass will show my life hacks to improve your circumstances now. Even if you feel that there is no hope.

www.ingramcontent.com/pod-product-compliance
Lightning Source LLC
Chambersburg PA
CBHW072010290426
44109CB00018B/2198